David Barrett's Harmonica Masterclass

Blues Harmonica Jam Tracks & Soloing Concepts #3

Level 3
Complete Blues Harmonica
Lesson Series

Online Audio www.melbay.com/99115BCDEB

1 2 3 4 5 6 7 8 9 0

Visit us on the Web at www.melbay.com — E-mail us at email@melbay.com

Contents & Audio Track List

Musicians: John Garcia, Vocals & Guitar; Steve Czarnecki, Organ; Steve Lucky, Piano; Randy Bermudes, Bass; and Paul Revelli, Drums.

Proof Readers: Thank you to Dennis Carelli and Diane Smith for proofreading.

A Word from the Author

Welcome to the *Harmonica Masterclass® Complete Blues Harmonica Lesson Series Level Three*. My name is David Barrett, and I'm the author of this lesson series. At this stage you should have already studied Level 1 and Level 2. Although this book and audio combination can stand on it's own, the studies found within the materials in this series (and the previous series) will help you tremendously in understanding the ideas covered in this book. It's highly recommended that you have already completed *Blues Harmonica Jam Tracks & Soloing Concepts #1* (MB99105M), *Blues Harmonica Jam Tracks & Soloing Concepts #2* (MB99110M), and one of the Exploring series books (*Exploring 2nd Position* MB99183M, *Exploring 3rd Position* MB99184M or *Exploring 1st Position* MB99185). Refer to the back of this book for details about the entire *Harmonica Masterclass Lesson Series*. If you have any questions regarding this book, or any other books within the series, look at the Harmonica Masterclass website at www.harmonicamasterclass.com, or contact me by mail at PO Box 1723, Morgan Hill, CA 95038.

Blues Harmonica Jam Tracks & Soloing Concepts #3

In book one we studied the twelve bar blues progression and became familiar with its common phrasing. The jam tracks presented songs in the most common keys, grooves and tempos played by professional blues musicians. In book two we studied introductions, breaks, endings and some soloing themes to help you be more innovative in your performing of long solos and instrumentals. The jam tracks presented songs that were faster, slower, in major and minor keys, and other various elements that the more advanced blues musician will encounter playing with a professional band. In the Exploring Series you studied Verse Forms (now called Chorus Forms), a key concept in soloing. You're now ready for book three.

Within this book we'll study: heads; hooks; bridges; unison playing, harmony playing; instrumental song construction and comping. The jam tracks present songs just as you would perform them live or on recording. Songs include: heads; breaks; bridges; unison and harmony playing with other musicians; areas for comping behind other musicians; and much more. All tracks are from my album with John Garcia *Serious Fun*. You'll find the musicianship and recording quality unparalleled in the jam track market.

As a special bonus I have included instrumental solos from guest artists' Gary Smith, R.J. Mischo, Gary Primich, Andy Just, Tom Ball, Joe Filisko, Mitch Kashmar and Mark Hummel. After completing this book and audio your next study is *Improvising Blues Harmonica* (MB20943M) and *Blues Harmonica Accompaniment Playing* (MB21385M). Good luck and enjoy your study!

Section 1 - A Word About Notation

The harmonica notation in this book is based on the ten hole diatonic harmonica played in first, second, or third position. Harmonica players use a wide variety of keyed harmonicas in their music. For ease of reading, all harmonica parts played on the ten hole diatonic harmonica will use the key signature of C major. This will place you in the pitch set of a C major harmonica. Through years of teaching, writing and conducting seminars, I have found this method of notation to be the fastest for translating musical thought. Diagrammed below is a C major ten hole diatonic harmonica.

BLOW ⟶	C	E	G	C	E	G	C	E	G	C
C	1	2	3	4	5	6	7	8	9	10
DRAW ⟶	D	G	B	D	F	A	B	D	F	A

Harmonica Tablature

You'll notice in the diagram that each hole has a corresponding number. In the tablature, the number corresponding to the hole will be under the notational symbol for the note to be played. When a note stands by itself, the note is to be drawn (inhaled). When a number is followed with a plus (+), the note is to be blown (exhaled). If the note is to be bent, a series of slashes will be notated to the right of the number. Each slash represents a half step bend. For example: three draw (3), bent down a half step, is "B-flat" and is notated as 3'. Three draw, bent down a whole step, is "A" and is notated as 3". Three draw, bent down a whole step and one half (minor third bend), is "A-flat" and is notated as 3'". Diagrammed below is the entire bend chart for a C major diatonic harmonica.

	1	2	3	4	5	6	7	8	9	10
Whole Step Bend (") →										B♭
½ Step Bend (') →								E♭	G♭	B
BLOW →	C	E	G	C	E	G	C	E	G	C
C	1	2	3	4	5	6	7	8	9	10
DRAW →	D	G	B	D	F	A	B	D	F	A
½ Step Bend (') →	D♭	G♭	B♭	D♭		A♭				
Whole Step Bend (") →		F	A							
1-½ Step Bend (''') →			A♭							

Rhythm

The rhythmic notation used is based on classical notational norms with the exception of the swinging of rhythms. Most rhythmic patterns played by a blues musician are swung. The word ***Swing*** means to take an eighth note pattern that would otherwise be played straight (1/2 beat & 1/2 beat = 1 beat) and elongates the first eighth (2/3) while shortening and placing the second eighth later in time relative to the first eighth (1/3) (2/3 & 1/3 = 1 beat). If the notation showed every part that is swung, instead of seeing two eighth notes together you would see three triplet eighths with the first two notes in the triplet figure tied together. This would crowd the music very quickly and make it difficult to read. You will not see any markers indicating that a rhythm is swung, it's always assumed.

Notation Specific to Harmonica Tablature

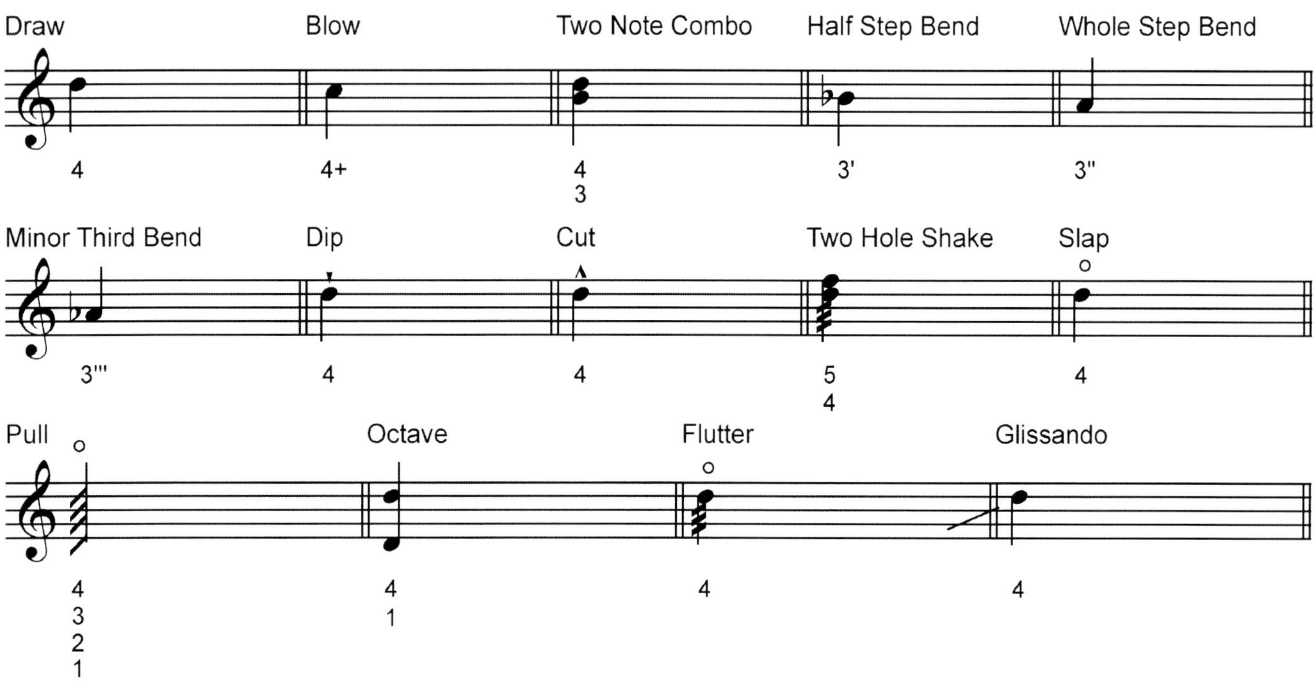

Section 2 – **Heads, Hooks & Bridges**

The Head

The ***Head*** is the main theme of your composition. The melody contained in the head is what the listener will come away with and what differentiates your song or instrumental from any other. The head is commonly the first chorus (twelve measures or one time through the form) heard, unless it's preceded by an opening. The head commonly comes back at the end of an instrumental to once again reinforce the head/melody and let the listener know you're finishing the song.

The main lick used for the head (**A**) should be rhythmically and melodically catchy. It's best to use repetitive Chorus Forms like **AAA**, **AAB** and **A B/A C**. A melody cannot be created without repetition. For this reason, it's also common to play the head twice at the open and close of an instrumental. Demonstrated below are head examples.

"Serious Fun"

This head uses the **A B/A C** Chorus Form and is doubled in unison by the guitar for a stronger presentation. Instrumental doubling (in unison or octaves) is very common for the head of a harmonica song.

2

"Don't Fight It"

This head uses the **AAB** Chorus Form and is doubled in unison by the guitar as well. You'll also hear the organ mimicking the line to add weight to the head. For this fast song it makes sense to use a more repetitive Chorus Form.

3

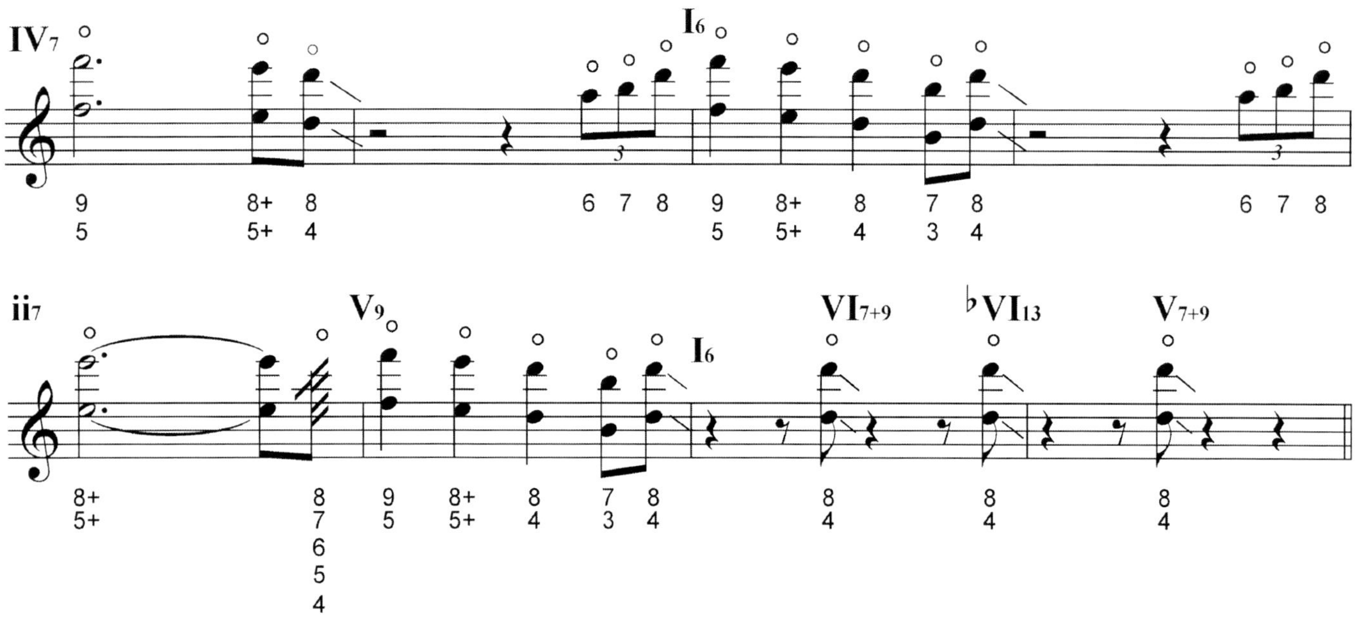

"Quiet World"
This head uses the **A B/A C** Chorus Form.

4

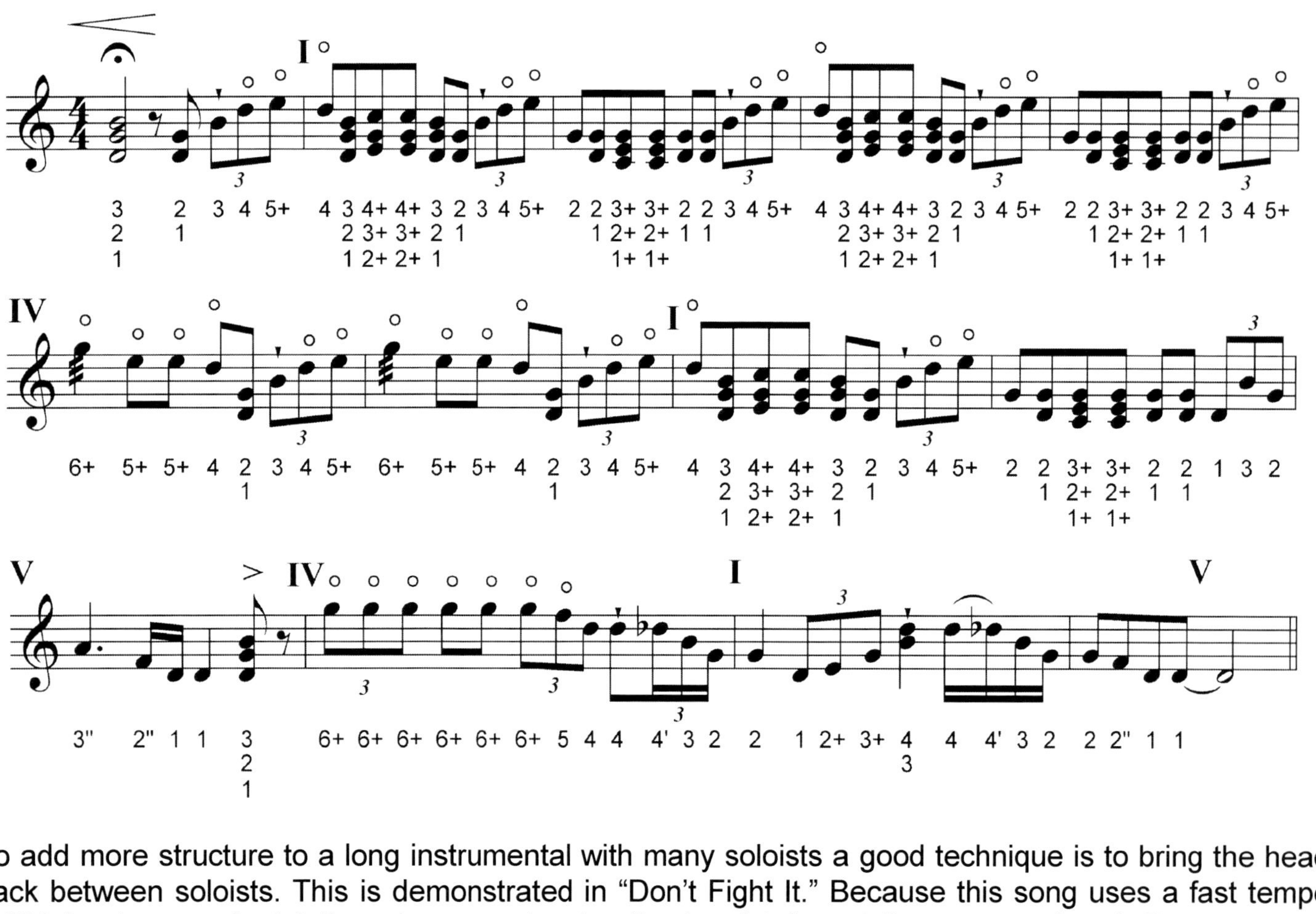

To add more structure to a long instrumental with many soloists a good technique is to bring the head back between soloists. This is demonstrated in "Don't Fight It." Because this song uses a fast tempo (~200 beats per minute) it made sense to play the head twice at the open and end. Demonstrated below is a chart of the song. The head is abbreviated as **H**.

| **H** | **H** | Harp Solo | **H** | Guitar Solo | **H** | Drum Solo | **H** | Piano Solo | **H** | Organ Solo | Harp/Gtr | **H** | **H** ||

In some cases two heads are better than one! In the song "Serious Fun" the first chorus is the main head. In the second chorus head two is played. Head two is used to launch the soloist. In this case head two is a four-measure phrase (**A**) played twice, with the last four measures (**B**) the new soloist taking over. The song also includes a bridge, though head two is the main call for the next soloist. At the end of the song head one comes back to finish.

Demonstrated below is a chart of the song. The bridge is abbreviated as **B**.

| **H1** | **H2** | Harp Solo | **B** | **H2** | Guitar Solo | **B** | **H2** | Organ Solo | Harp/Guitar Solo | **H1** ||

You can see and hear the importance the head plays in a composition. Start working on writing heads now. All you need to have in a live performance to make a song memorable is a good head. If you like to go to jam sessions or you are often called up by bands to play with them for a number or two—this is your chance to shine! Instead of saying "I'll just play with you" when the bandleader says "what do you want to do," you can say "shuffle in F, from the one" and count them in knowing you can create a great instrumental on the spot. All you need is a head. A song without a head is just a jam... nothing memorable for the listener to walk away with.

Try it this way. Play a head you worked on ahead of time with a jam track. It's going to sound good because you worked it out over and over until you were really happy with it. Take a solo after the head and come back to the head before handing over the solo to the guitarist. When he's done, play the head again and solo for a while. When it feels right, play the head again and take the song out. Now that's a song the audience will remember! This is demonstrated below.

| **H** | **H** | Harp Solo | **H** | Guitar Solo | **H** | Harp Solo | **H** ||

The construction of a head almost always starts with a catchy lick. I'm sure you've played a lick that you made up that you felt really good about. When a lick like that comes up, apply the Chorus Forms (different ways in which to repeat that lick within one chorus) to find which Chorus Form presents your lick the best. Work with it over and over until you are pleased with all the elements within the head. You don't have to work out the solos. Most instrumentals the head is the only element of the solo premeditated. If you feel more comfortable working out the solos as well, that's fine. The main point here is start working on heads so that you can pull one out at any moment to match the mood of the audience and skill level of the band. Later in the text I will show you an example of how an instrumental was born from one lick in the song "Lick Train."

Listed below are instrumentals worth checking out for their use of the head. Of course there are many more good examples than this list offers, but this is a good start.

- "Juke" by Little Walter – Head is played at opening and doesn't come back at end. Head uses the **AAB** Chorus Form.
- "Cotton Creeper" by James Cotton – Depending on which version you hear, the head is commonly played twice at the opening and comes back throughout the solo between break sections. Head uses the **ABC** Chorus Form for the opening two choruses and **A B/A C** for the return of the head between break sections.
- "Easy" by Big Walter Horton – In this song the head is played for three choruses with a deviation at the fourth chorus for a nice solo and comes back to the head at the end. Head uses the **ABC** Chorus Form.
- "Hand Jive" by Mark Hummel – Head is played twice after intro and once at end. Head is similar to **A B/A C** Chorus Form.
- "The Upsetter" by Rod Piazza – Head is played twice at open and once at end. Head uses the **ABC** Chorus Form.
- "Gibson Creek Shuffle" by Mark Ford – Head is played twice at open and twice at the end. Guitar plays unison with harmonica. Head uses the **A B/A C** Chorus Form.
- "Fogtown Swing" by Gary Smith – Head is played once at beginning and end. Head uses the **A B/A C** Chorus Form. Guitar doubles the harmonica in unison for the head until the **V** chord where the guitar takes over.

- "Red Top" covered by Gary Primich – A cool Jazz tune with the head played twice at open and twice at the end. Head uses the **A B/A C** Chorus Form.
- "Chicken Shack" by Jimmy Smith – A great jazz tune that has been adopted by many harmonica players (Little Walter and Charlie Musselwhite to name two). Head is played twice at the open and twice at the end. Head uses the **A B/A C** Chorus Form.
- "Watermelon Man" by Herbie Hancock – A true jazz tune using blues changes. Head is played twice at the open and twice at the end. Head is similar to **AA^{1}B** Chorus Form.

The Hook

The head is the main theme of your composition, one chorus in length, played over a groove presented by the rhythm section. The head is commonly played at the beginning and ending of a song. The ***Hook*** is the main theme of your composition, up to four measures in length (usually one or two measures) and is played throughout the song. The hook is a small, catchy lick or phrase that permeates the entire song. Because the hook is played the entire song, it's usually played by the rhythm section, but this is not always the case.

Being that the hook is small, it's usually sequenced over all the chord changes (notes are changed to match the chord they are played over, but the line retains its contour, rhythm and placement within the chord). This concept is demonstrated well in "Chicago Style" by John Garcia. Notated below is the bass and guitar pattern, played an octave apart. Even though this is a common groove, because of its prominence in the song it can be considered a hook.

This song also has a hook played by the second rhythm guitar and harmonica. I'm playing a Low D harmonica in an octave embouchure to get a more horn-like tone. I would recommend you learn this line for later use; I use permutations of this line often in background playing. Notation for this passage is shown below.

5

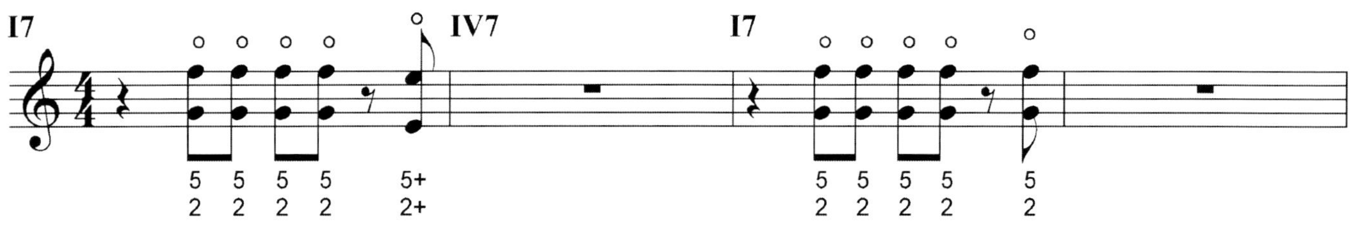

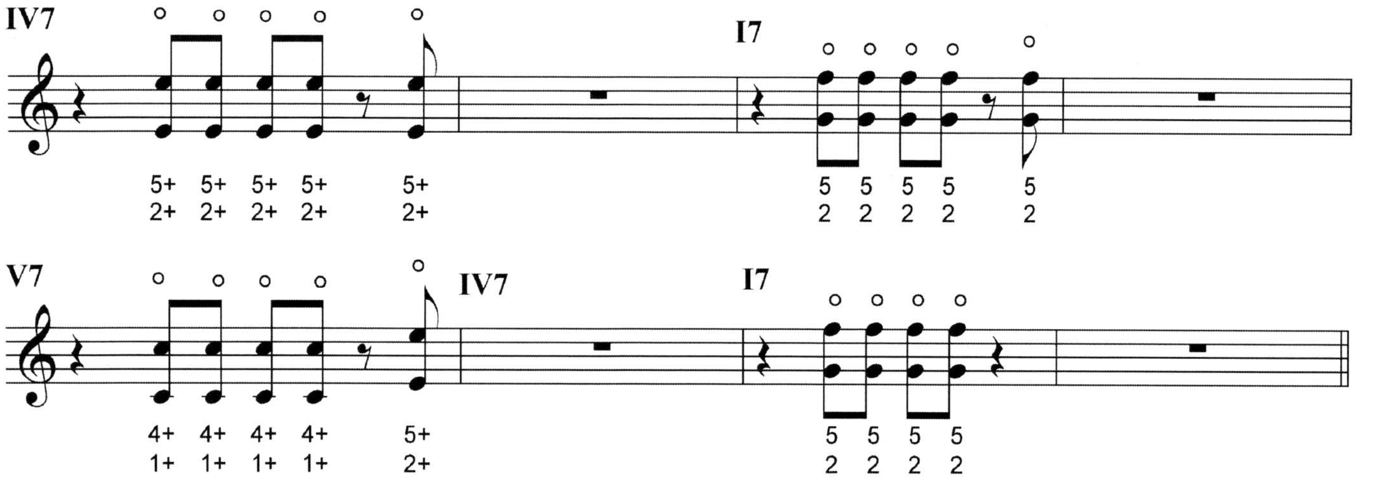

Finally, this song also has a head. It's not common for a song to have a strong hook and a head, let alone two hooks and a head, but it works for this song. Listen to the recorded example and separate in your mind the three distinct elements. Also notice that the head is played twice at the opening before the bridge and then the harmonica solo.

Listed on the following page are songs worth checking out for their use of a hook. Again, there are many more good examples than this list offers, but this is a good start.

- "Blues With A Feeling" by Little Walter – Hook is the first lick played and is repeated in a **A B/A C** Chorus Form. This hook is then played at every vocal break. This is a good example of how a piece of the head is used throughout a song to create a nice hook.
- "Cotton Creeper" by James Cotton – After the head is played, the song moves to a break section. The first line played is the hook. This hook is a small rhythmic line played on the 4 draw.
- "I'm Ready" covered by Muddy Waters – Nice strong hook that harmonica, guitar and bass cover, sequenced over all chord changes. An example of what you could play on the harp is notated below.

6

As accompaniment players, the hook is a great line for us to grab onto and play. Being a prominent line in a composition, it makes sense to add weight to it by playing the line in unison or harmony. This is a good time for us to now cover how to play harmonies.

Playing Accompaniment within the Chord

The concept of harmony playing is simple. Play a note, any note within the range of the harmonica that is within the chord you're playing over and it will match. Demonstrated below are the chord changes for the song "Chicago Style." The song is in the key of A using a D harmonica in second position. As in prior texts we'll always think as if we're playing in G, using a C harmonica. Since the harmonicas do the transposing for us, this allows us to become fluid with theory concepts much faster.

If you have memorized the notes available on your C harmonica with bends (you have done that, right?), this study is easy. If you're playing over the **I7** chord, then you can hit any G, B, D, or F on the range of your instrument. For those that have not memorized these notes, detailed below is a chart. The left column contains the notes of the **I7** chord—you can play any of these holes over the **I7** chord. The middle column contains the notes of the **IV7** chord—you can play any of these holes over the **IV7** chord. The right column contains the notes of the **V7** chord—you can play any of these holes over the **V7** chord.

I7	IV7	V7
1	**1+**	**1+/1**
2"/2	**2+/2**	**2'**
3	**3+/3'**	**3"**
4	**4+**	**4+/4**
5	**5+**	**-**
6+	**6+**	**6**
7	**7+**	**7+**
8	**8+**	**8**
9	**9+**	**(9'+)**
9+	**(10"+)/10+**	**10/10+**
(10'+)		

Play any combination of these notes you wish to the recorded jam track "Chicago Style." Demonstrated on the following page is what I played on the original recording.

The notes that have the most texture are the thirds and sevenths of each chord. For the **I7** chord the notes are B and F. For the **IV7** chord the notes are E and B-flat. For the **V7** chord the notes are F-sharp and C. Notice in my version of the hook in this piece I play the root (G) and seventh (F) in an octave embouchure for the **I7** chord, I play the third (E) in an octave for the **IV7** chord and I play the seventh (C) in an octave for the **V7** chord.

Harmony Playing with Another Instrument

To play in harmony with another instrument, including a harmonica player, follow the same procedure. It's actually quite simple to do once you become familiar with the chord tones of the three common chords. As a general rule try to be as conjunct as possible in your movement among chord change. In other words, if you start on a 2 draw for the **I7** chord, the next note for the **IV7** chord should stay on the same hole or a nearby hole. In the case of the **IV7** chord you can stay on the 2 draw (G, which is the fifth of the chord) or move to 2 blow (E, which is the third of the chord). This is demonstrated below.

7

The Bridge

The ***Bridge*** is a deviation from the form that commonly links two sections together. The deviation in form can come from a change in the length of the form, a change in the chords used in the form or most commonly both. A common example is to go to an eight bar blues for the bridge in a song that uses a 12 bar form. The vocal bridge will commonly go after two vocal verses then followed by a instrumental solo. In this case the bridge is helping to transition from the main vocal verse to the solo. In an instrumental the bridge is commonly used to transition from one soloist to the next.

For this study let's look at the song "Serious Fun." Detailed below is the chart for this song.

| **H1** | **H2** | Harp Solo | **B** | **H2** | Guitar Solo | **B** | **H2** | Organ Solo | **B** | **H2** | Harp/Gtr | **H1** ||

In this song the bridge comes at the end of a solo. The bridge then leads into the return of head two and ultimately a new soloist. The song uses a standard 12 bar form, with the bridge moving to an 8 bar form. The chord changes for the 8 bar section are below. Listening to the sample you'll hear the **II7** chord adds harmonic change for nice effect.

8

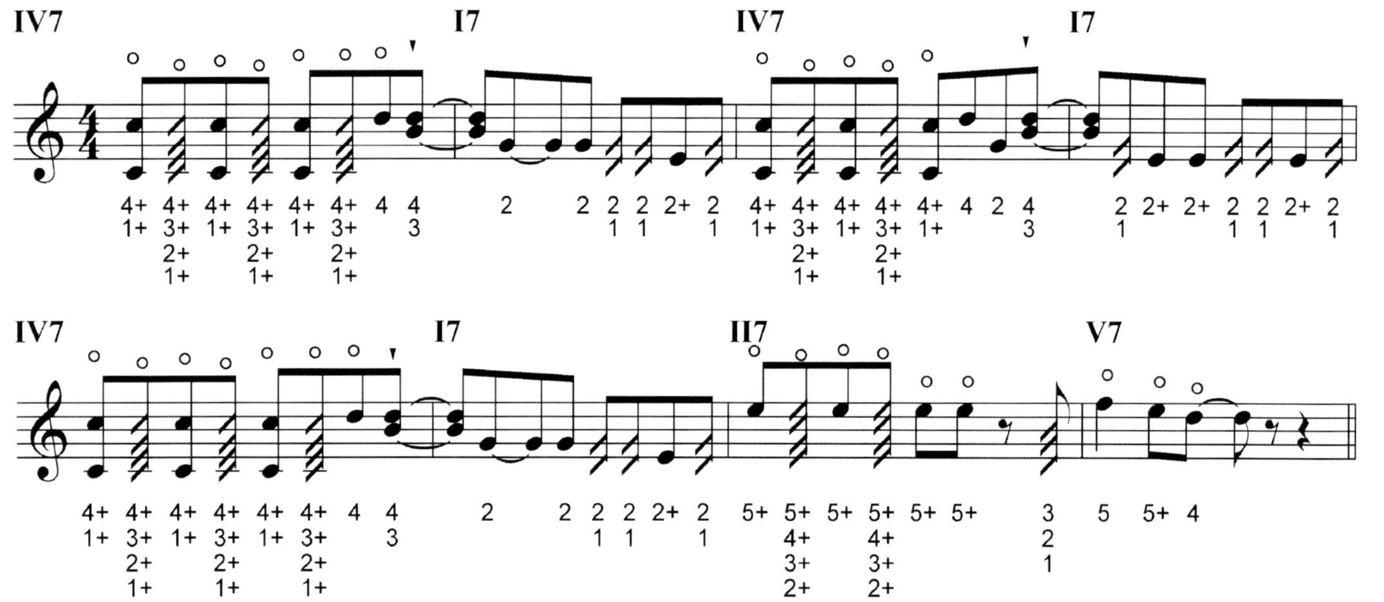

Blues has the potential to get old quickly due to its repetitive form. Bridges and breaks within a song are a relative easy way to add some spice. Listen to the next example from "Chicago Style." In this case the bridge does not deviate from the form in any way except for the break and a four-measure unison line played by the guitar, organ and harmonica. Listen to how the bridge sets up the next soloist nicely.

9

Section 3 – **Non-12 Bar Blues Chord Change Challenges**

In *Scales, Patterns and Bending Exercises #2* (MB99112M) we studied how to construct all of the common chords and learned how to find the notes of these chords on the harmonica. Let's use John Garcia's song "A Real Romance" to put your skills to the test. Let's start by identifying the chords used in the verse and bridge of the song. Detailed below is a chord chart of the song.

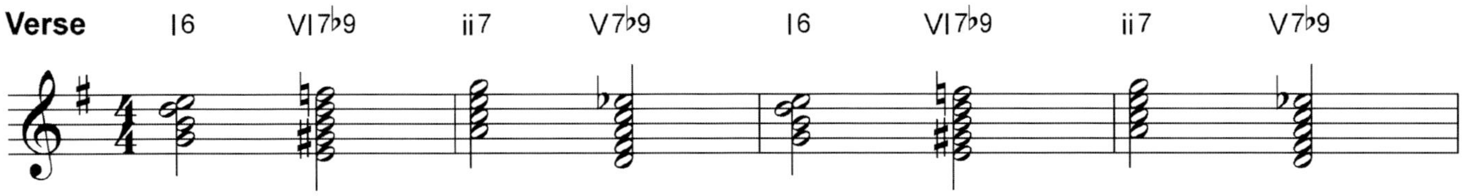

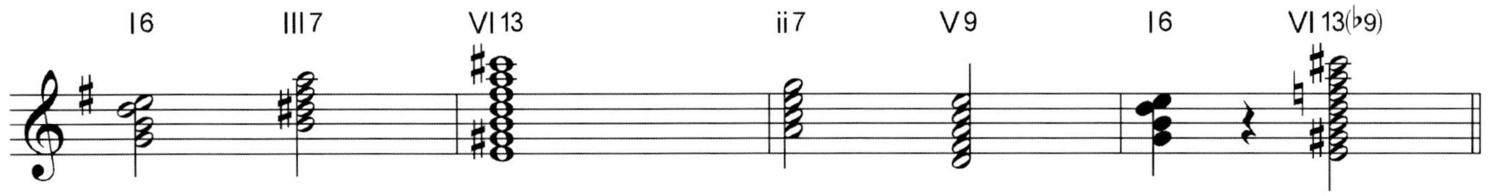

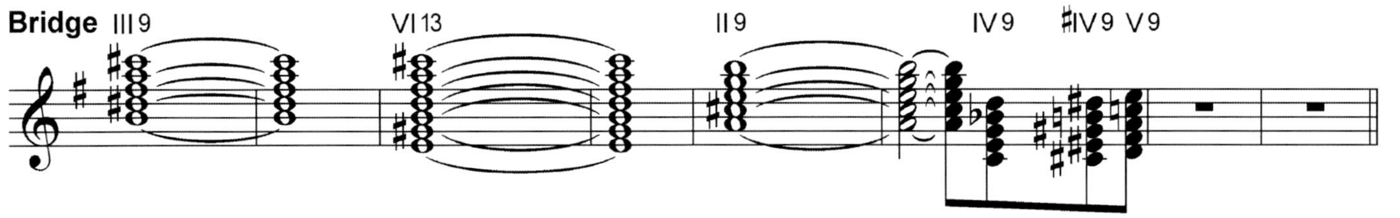

Now let's list all of the pitches as if we were playing on a C harmonica in the key of G (second position). Now that you know the notes within the chord, you know what notes can be safely used within each chord (use the harmonica note chart on page 4 if you haven't memorized the pitches on your C harmonica). Be aware that playing chord tones beyond the ninth can get dissonant. Experiment with different chord tones until you find combinations that allow conjunct movement.

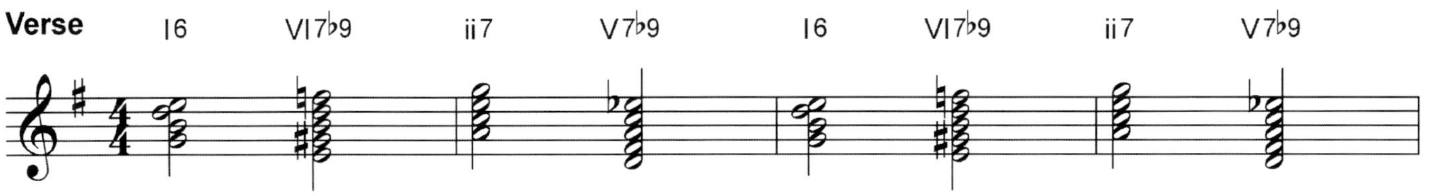

I6	VI7♭9	ii7	V7♭9	I6	VI7♭9	ii7	V7♭9
E	F	G	E♭	E	F	G	E♭
D	D	E	C	D	D	E	C
B	B	C	A	B	B	C	A
G	G♯	A	F♯	G	G♯	A	F♯
	E		D		E		D

I6	III7	VI13	ii7	V9	I6	VI13(♭9)
E	A	C♯	G	E	E	C♯
D	F♯	A	E	C	D	A
B	D♯	F♯	C	A	B	F
G	B	D	A	F♯	G	D
		B		D		B
		G♯				G♯
		E				E

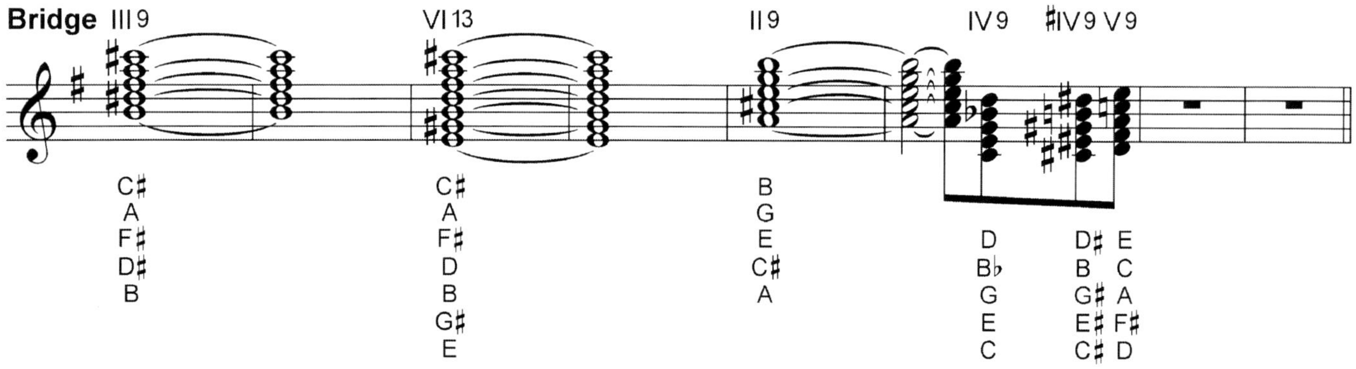

Notated below are the notes I chose to use for backing the vocals. Notice the conjunct movement of the harp lines. For the **I** chord I played the root (G), the **VI** chord I used the root (E), the **ii** chord I used the fifth (E) and the **V** chord I used the root (D). Playing roots, thirds and fifths help give the song a more major sound. Later in the piece I use flat-sevenths and ninths to add interest. Use the chord charts above to give you some safe notes and experiment with what sounds good to you. Using notes between chord tones (called passing tones) will help to make your lines more fluid. Feel free to experiment with any note combination that sounds good to you. Just remember, chord tones are a safe haven if you don't have any ideas on what to do or your lines consistently come out with a couple stinker notes.

10

Our next example is what I played for the solo. It took me a while to work out the solo for this song. Because the chord changes are different than anything I've ever played, it was a challenge to come up with something fluid. I worked out ideas with John a couple times and he would say "It's OK, but it sounds like you're playing too much by the numbers." Translated… I was playing too cautious and it didn't sound inspired. I worked the solo over and over until I fell into some patterns I liked. Challenge yourself with the jam track to this song to create a solo you like. The more you take challenges on like this the better you'll be able to handle pieces in the future.

11

Section 4 – Song Construction Example w/Special Guests

Now that you're within level three you're probably playing with people and trying to improve your performance and writing skills. Writing an instrumental can be a huge challenge at first, so let's take a moment and look at an example. I'll now walk you through the process I went through to write the song "Lick Train" on the album.

I had a purpose in mind when I wrote this song. I was invited to participate in a blues harmonica blowout while I was on the road with the Harmonica Masterclass Workshop. I started working on a new song to play for the show. I wanted the song to start with harmonica playing a strong rhythmic lick over the **I** chord that really caught the ear of the audience that this song was going to kick butt! The band would then come in on the **IV** chord with a shuffle. That's where it started. The main lick I came up with was pretty standard, but the techniques used were tried and tested through the years to have the quality I was looking for. Notated below is the lick.

12

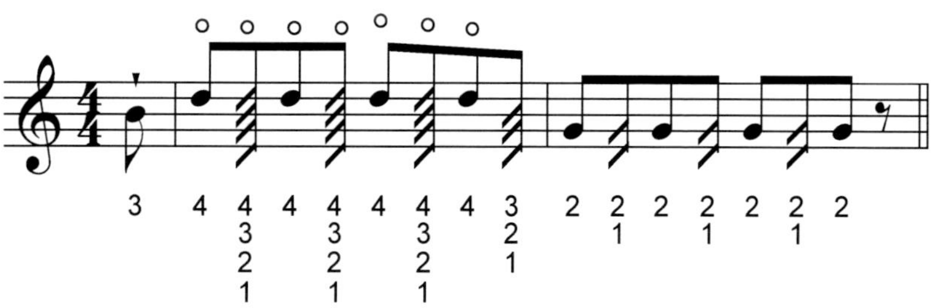

I worked on the head over and over until I came up with what's notated below.

13

This head is busier than I would normally write, but it worked. From there I worked on what I would do in the body of the instrumental. I wanted more breaks to make what could be a normal shuffle in E stand out. As I worked on ideas I came up with using the same rhythm and technique approach of the head in an ascending pattern. This is notated below.

14

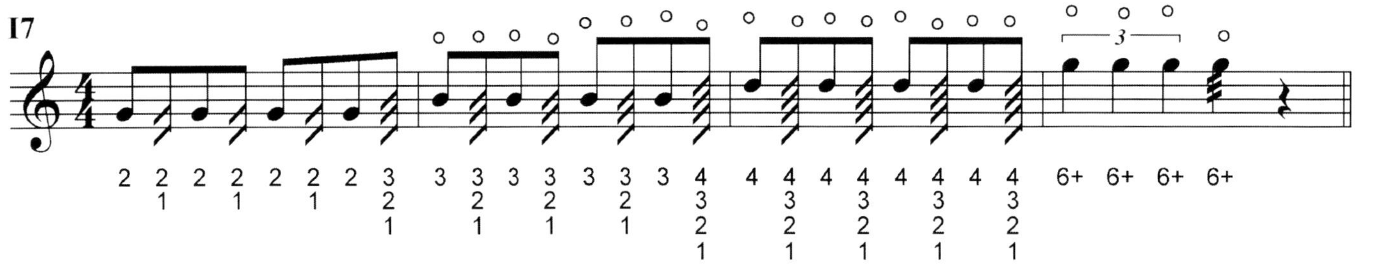

From there I played the same line one octave higher. This worked out well because it gave me a logical way to move to the high end and the upper octaves present themselves well for the big tone I was trying to achieve for this piece. This is notated below.

15

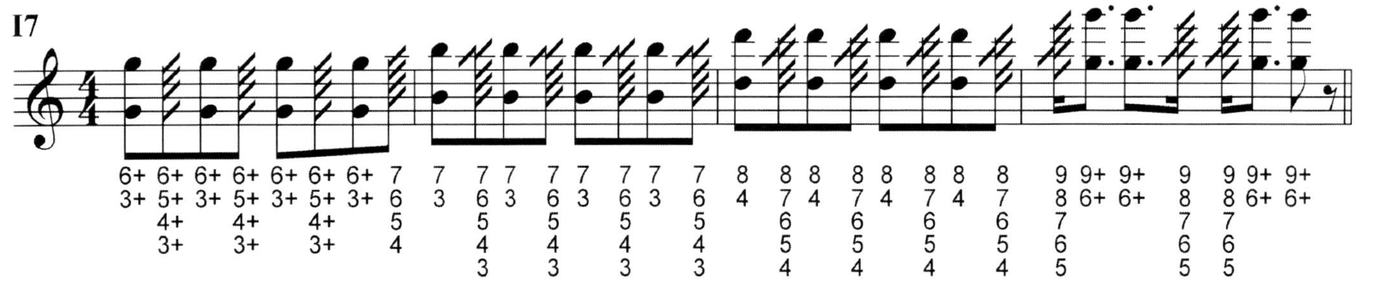

At that time I thought it would be cool to have a piece that used breaks every chorus. I quickly decided against that idea due to the two prior ascending lines used the note range of the harmonica up very quickly. I soon settled on the idea of using these ascending lines between solo sections. This is demonstrated below.

| **H** | **H** | ? | ? | Ascending Line #1 | ? | ? | Ascending Line #2 | ? | …

Again, because of how much range was being used so quickly I decided to make the song short and sweet and came up with the song form below.

| **H** | **H** | ? | Ascending Line #1 | ? | Ascending Line #2 | **H** ||

The head was pretty active and so was the first ascending line. I decided to play something low on the harmonica that used more drawn out notes. The first ascending line brought me to the mid range of the harmonica so I decided to stay there and play something on the 2/5 after it. Ascending line two didn't leave much room to do anything else so I went back to the head to finish it. After playing it a couple times, the head at the end sounded anticlimactic so I worked on some ideas and eventually went with a line that sprang from the first four measures that brought me to the high end to climax with a 10+ to 10"+ lick. It felt a little over-the-top at first when practicing it, but in the end I felt it was the right thing to play. When performing in a series of Mark Hummel harmonica blowout shows that included Paul deLay, Paul gave me friendly grief about the high-end note. Rock 'n' Roll harmonica players have in the past over-used that little lick (most notably the famous Magic Dick solo "Whammer Jammer").

Notated on the following page is the final outcome of the song "Lick Train." Below is the final chart.

| **H** | **H** | Solo 12 | Break-Ascending Line #1 | Solo 12 | Break-Ascending Line #2 | **H** ||

24

Lick Train

A Harmonica, 2nd Position (Key of E)

By David Barrett from the Album "Serious Fun" with John Garcia.

Chorus 1 (Head) Listen for common additions of upper notes (ex. 4 with 5) and standard 3 draw quartertone usage.

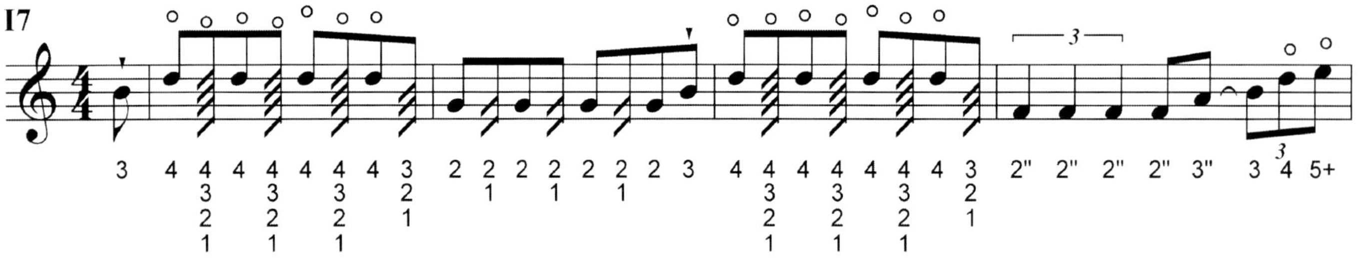

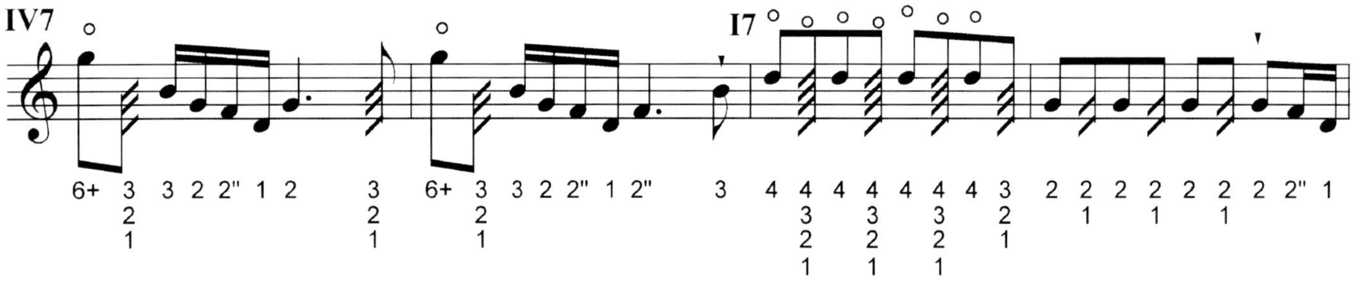

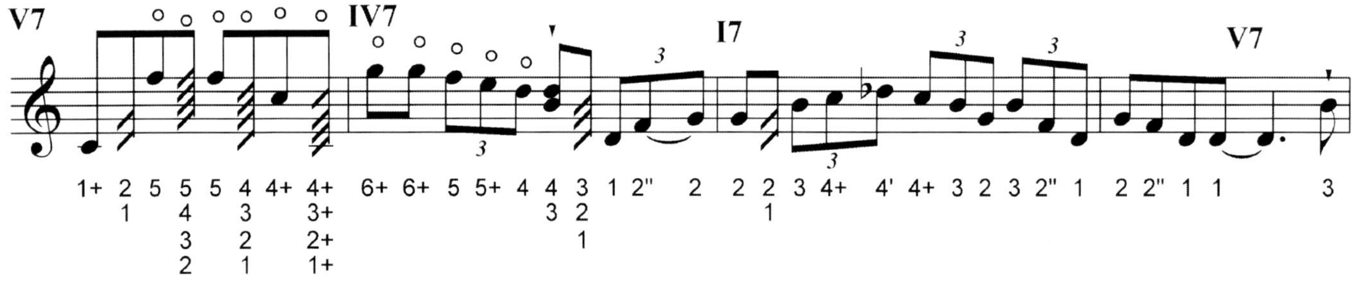

Chorus 2 (Head)

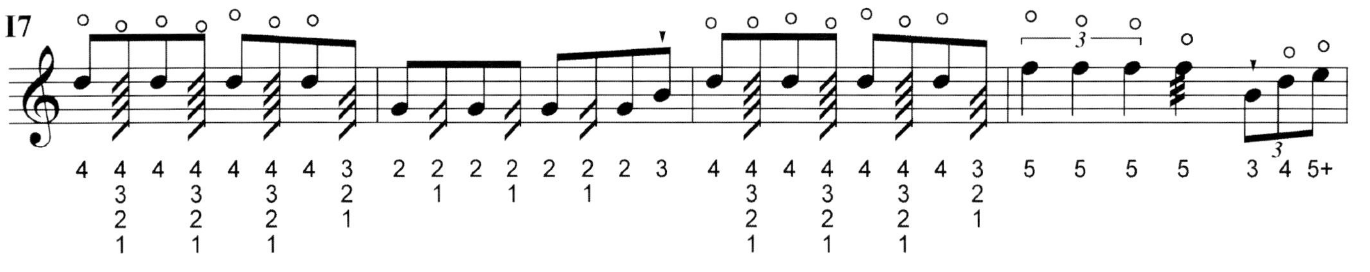

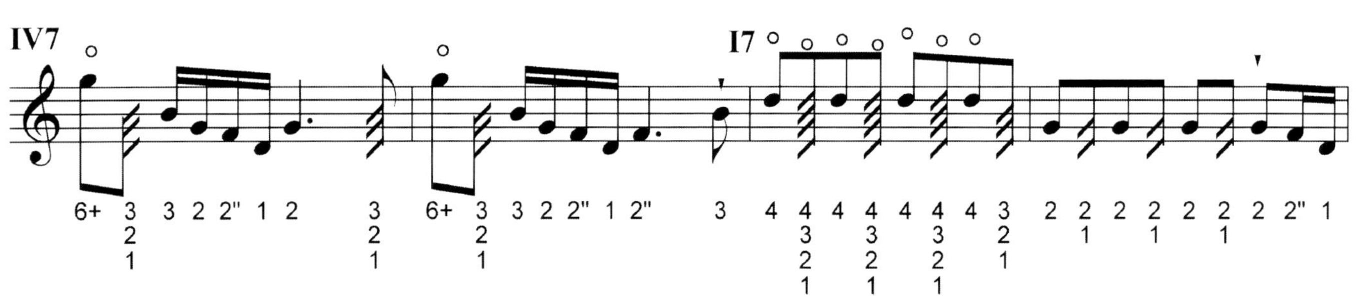

V7
IV7
I7
V7
Chorus 3
I7
IV7
I7
V7
IV7
I7
V7
Chorus 4
I7
IV7
I7

V7
IV7
I7
V7
Chorus 5
I7
Add a little of upper note
IV7
I7
V7
IV7
I7
V7
Chorus 6
I7
IV7
I7

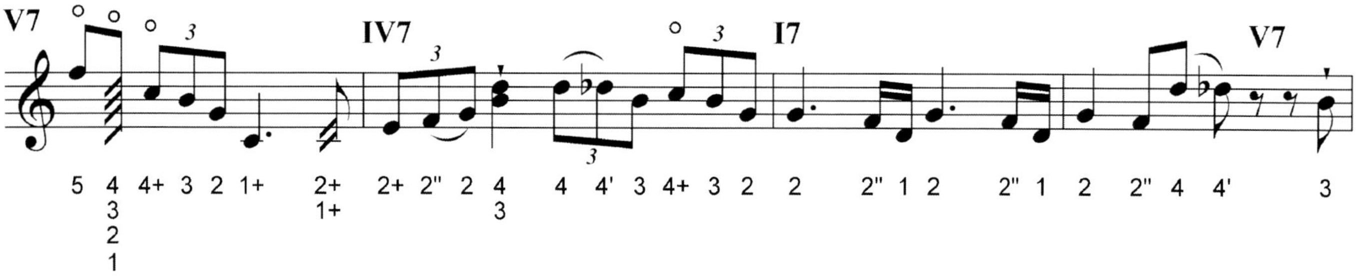

Chorus 7 (Head)

Now that you've heard my version, let the fun begin! The following audio examples showcase well-known blues harmonica players performing an instrumental to the "Lick Train" backing track. As friends came through the San Francisco, California Bay Area on tour I invited them to come and record at my School of the Blues in San Jose for this epic project. I told each artist they could spend as much time as they want to work out their ideas for the song, but they could not hear my original or what the other artists' have done before them. The goal was that each artist had a fresh perspective on the performance of their instrumental. I was, as you will probably be, pleasantly surprised with the differences on how each player approached this song. Some chose to play amplified, others acoustic. Some played a head that came back at the end, others didn't. Not only is this great fun to listen to, it's a great exercise in how there are endless options on how a song can be performed. Detailed below are the artists that recorded and some notes on what they did. After the artists' recorded examples you'll hear the original "Lick Train" as performed by me again for comparison.

16 Gary Smith

Gary was my teacher at age 16 and was a huge influence on my playing and teaching. He has recorded many albums through the years and is getting more and more recognized for the master he is. Gary can commonly be found gigging in the San Francisco/San Jose Bay Area. Gary starts on the **IV** chord with the band and uses the first chorus as an intro. The second chorus starts in the break (four measures) with what he comes back to on the final chorus and can be considered the theme, or a loose head. For the third chorus notice the nice Elmore James "Dust my Broom" quote. The fourth chorus he quotes the hook to James Cotton's instrumental "Creeper." For the fifth chorus notice the nice use of the 2 blow on the **IV** chord (third of the chord). For the final chorus he comes back to the lines used in the second chorus break and finishes the song. Gary used my silver-face Fender Princeton Reverb amp (1967 I believe) and old Shure mic with a Controlled Reluctance element. The amp was mic'd with a Shure SM57 about one inch back and one inch in from the outside rim of the speaker.

17 R.J. Mischo

R.J., originally from Milwaukee, has been in the San Francisco Bay Area for many years and is a fantastic performer and songwriter in our area and abroad. R.J. can be heard on many major labels, including the European Crosscut Records label. You'll notice he's very influenced by Sonny Boy Williamson's style. R.J. starts with the same style of swinging rhythm as I did for the opening on the 2 draw. That's where the similarity ends. Notice the great kiss-pop technique used on the fourth chorus. For the fifth chorus he uses a nice Big Walter Horton "Walter's Boogie" type line. Over all, R.J. employs a nice use of range and hand effects. R.J. didn't use a head, though the 2 draw is brought in often as a reoccurring theme. R.J. played through a studio condenser mic directly into the board (recording console).

18 Gary Primich

Gary has been on the scene for many, many years with a very cool style all his own. From down-home blues albums to slick recordings with background singers and horn sections, he's done it all. Gary is a very active performer around the US and abroad; there's a good chance you can catch him in your area soon. Gary starts on the **IV** chord with the band. The second chorus starts with a nice chordal pattern played on the 2 draw. Notice the use of space in his playing; Gary never overdoes it. Gary has a very cool 6 draw line that he plays on the fifth chorus and the last chorus over the **V** chord. Gary used my Princeton amp with his Astatic mic. The amp was mic'd the same as mentioned above.

19 Andy Just

Along with fronting his own band, Andy is notably known for his touring and recorded work with the Ford Blues Band. Andy is also a very popular player in Australia. Andy's huge sound with a rock-like tone makes him stand out from the rest of the traditional blues harmonica players. Andy starts on the **I** chord with a 2 draw chordal pattern and leads the band in with a strong 4 draw. For the third chorus notice the nice use of bullet mic muting. Notice the nursery line quote used on the fourth chorus. Andy really digs in for a strong horn line on the fifth chorus. For the final chorus he returns to the 2 draw chordal pattern on the **I** to give the song a sense of a head. Andy used a Roland Cube amp, a Shure mic (controlled magnetic cartridge) and Digitech Valve FX signal processor.

20 Tom Ball

Tom was a great addition to the lineup due to his style of playing being so uniquely different. Tom's most known for his many albums, tours, TV and radio appearances with Kenny Sultan. Along with his performing and recording, Tom is an accomplished author of harmonica lesson material. Tom starts on the **IV** chord and plays a line that matches that of the lead guitar part. Cool idea. Tom plays the **IV** chord with a D harmonica, returning to the **I** chord with the A harmonica (both in second position). Notice Tom's strong use of hand effects and rhythmic patterns. Listen to the nice jumping line on the **IV** chord of the third chorus. For the fourth chorus Tom uses some nice lines on the high-end of the harmonica for the **IV** chord and plays a **V-IV-I** quote from Jerry McCain's song "Steady" that leads to a Sonny Terry style lick. "Steady" is quoted again through to the next chorus. The head is played again at the final chorus, lead by a great high-end lick. Notice the cool 3 draw/4 draw bent shake for the final note. Tom played through a studio condenser mic.

21 Joe Filisko

Joe is not only the world's premier diatonic harmonica customizer, he's a fantastic teacher and player as well. Because "Lick Train" is in the key of E, it makes position playing other than second position difficult for this song. Joe stepped to the plate and used a Low D harmonica in third position. What stands out most in Joe's playing is his tasty use of texture and dynamics. The first chorus is his head. The second chorus introduces a second head. The fourth chorus he plays a nice **I** chord arpeggio (1, 2', 3") in the break. This is hard to control on a regular tuned harmonica, let alone a Low D! Notice that head one and two return at the end of the song. Joe used a Marine Band Low D with an EV 605 mic and a Harmony amp model H189 with a whopping six-inch speaker.

22 Mitch Kashmar

Mitch is another stellar harmonica player that you're going to get the pleasure to listen to. Mitch is known for his singing/harp playing with the Pontiax blues band and mutual recordings with William Clarke. Mitch currently performs up and down the West Coast. Mitch starts big with a 3/4 (3 draw and 4 draw) combination, moving to a 4/5 combination. Take note of the **V-IV-I** lick (9th arpeggio) that he plays and repeats throughout the instrumental as a motif. For the fourth chorus he opens with a nice percussive draw chord. The fifth chorus he steps up to a 5/6 shake to build in pitch. The sixth chorus he uses a very nice repetitive (**AAB**) 4 draw lick. The song ends with a variation of the opening lick. Mitch used my Kalamazoo Model One amp with a 10" Jensen speaker (originally came with a 8" speaker) and Shure mic. After recording, I sent the recorded signal back into my Princeton to warm up the tone a little bit and add spring reverb. This is called re-micing.

23 Mark Hummel

Mark is one of the most active performers in the blues scene today with dates each year all around the world. His harmonica blowout shows are legendary and with over ten albums it's hard to not find his recordings in your local music store's blues section. Mark starts with a nice rhythmic lick, leading to a strong triplet pattern on the second chorus. Notice Mark's great use of space between ideas. Mark plays a nice quote on the sixth chorus and a great ascending lick on the final chorus. Mark used my Princeton amp and Shure mic. The amp was mic'd with a Shure SM57 about one inch back and one inch in from the outside rim of the speaker and a studio condenser mic about five feet away from the amp (known as a room or ambient mic). The room mic was balanced louder in the mix than the direct mic.

24 David Barrett

Now that you have listened to all these great players, here's my original cut from the album. Since I was in a large studio when recording the album, my setup was a little different. I recorded with the same Shure mic that the other players used. I used the same Princeton as well, though it was chained to a Fender 1959 Reissue Bassman modified by Sonny Jr. Along with mics up close, I used a couple room mics to balance the sound between the two amps and to get more of a room sound.

Section 5 – **Study Exercises**

Listed below are study exercises I have prepared for each section of this book. These are the same exer-cises I use with my private students; they have proven to be very helpful.

1. Write ten licks and apply the Chorus Forms to all of the licks. After playing them all, decide which chorus stands out to you as being the catchiest. Select a jam track to play with that matches the feel and tempo you're looking for. Play the head at the beginning of the song and at the end. Improvise all the choruses in the middle.
2. Write a simple chorus that uses lines that are horn-like in sound. Record yourself playing to a jam track. Locate the notes relative to the chord they are played over. For each note you played find a note within the chord that's close to it and write it down. What you end up with is the harmony part to your original line. For notes not found within the chord, experiment with different notes until the harmony sounds right.

Section 6 – **Blues Harmonica Jam Tracks**

The following songs are from the album *Serious Fun* by John Garcia and myself. Each of the songs have the harmonica parts removed. I have included a quick chart for each song and notation for any heads or hooks played. The musicians who performed on the album are: John Garcia: Vocals & Guitar, Steve Czarnecki: Organ, Steve Lucky: Piano, Randy Bermudes: Bass, and Paul Revelli: Drums.

25 Serious Fun **by David Barrett**

Key of Song: E Major Tempo: ~120 Harmonica: A Harmonica in 2nd Position

Groove: Shuffle Form: Standard 12 Bar Instrumentation: Full Band

Chart: | **H1** | **H2** | Harp x3 | **B** (8) | **H2** | Gtr x3 | **B** | **H2** | Organ x3 | **B** | **H2** | Harp/Gtr x2 | **H1** ||

Head 1

Head 2

Guitar & Harmonica Harmony Line – Track time: 6:25

Ending Line – Track time: 7:33

26 "Lick Train" by David Barrett

Key of Song: E Major Tempo: ~126 Harmonica: A Harmonica in 2nd Position

Groove: Shuffle Form: Standard 12 Bar Instrumentation: Full Band

Chart: | **H** | **H** | Solo | Break-IV | Solo | Break-IV | **H** ||

27 "Pretty Girls Everywhere" by E. Church, T. Williams

Key of Song: B-flat Major Tempo: ~120 Harmonica: A-flat Harmonica in 3rd Position (or E-flat in 2nd)

Groove: Rhumba Form: Standard 12 Bar Instrumentation: Full Band

Chart: | Open from V | Vocals x3 | Piano x2 | Vocals x2 | Gtr x2 | Vocals x3 | Harp x2+Fade ||

V-IV-I Hook

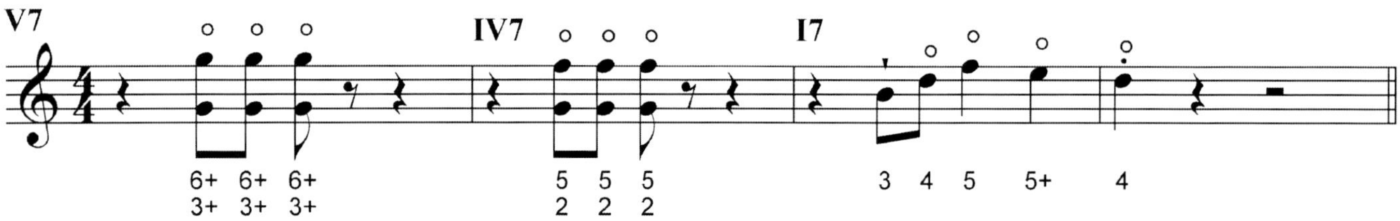

28 "Chicago Style" by John Garcia

Key of Song: A Major Tempo: ~116 Harmonica: Standard and Low D Harmonica in 2nd Position

Groove: Chicago Shuffle Form: Standard 12 Bar Instrumentation: Full Band

Chart: | **H** | **H** | **B**/Break to Harp x3 | **B**/Break to Organ x3 | **H** | **B**/Break to Gtr = x5+Fade ||

Low D Hook – Entire song except for first chorus of each solo.

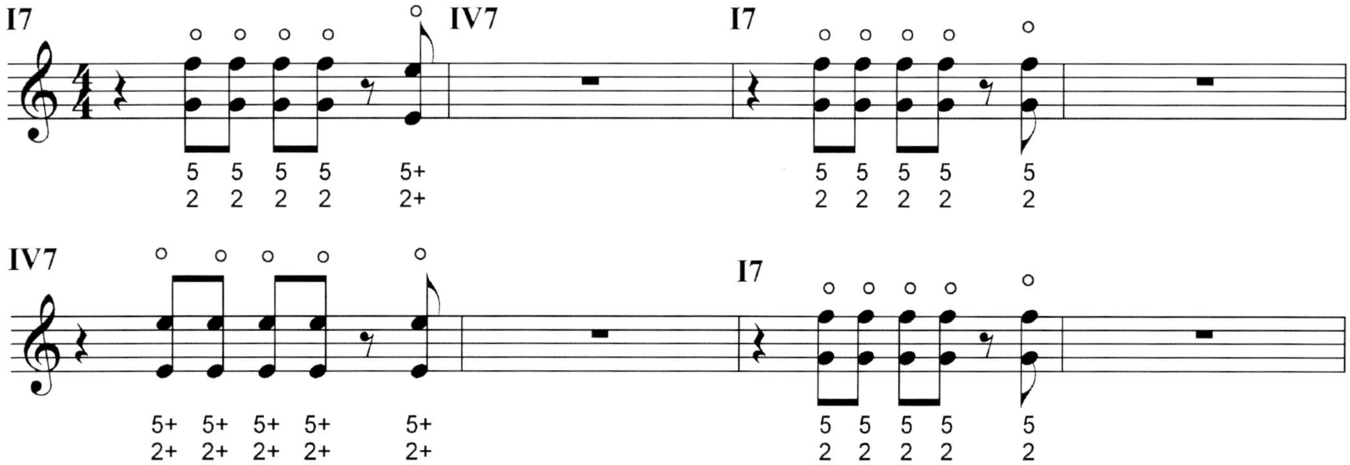

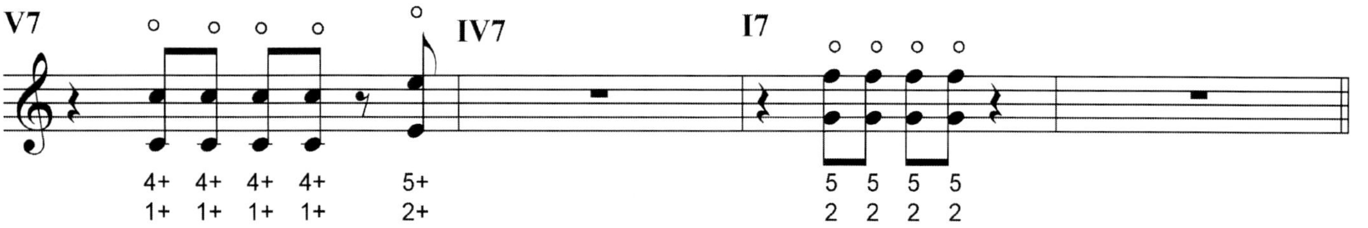

Low D Bridge Hook – Track time: 0:51

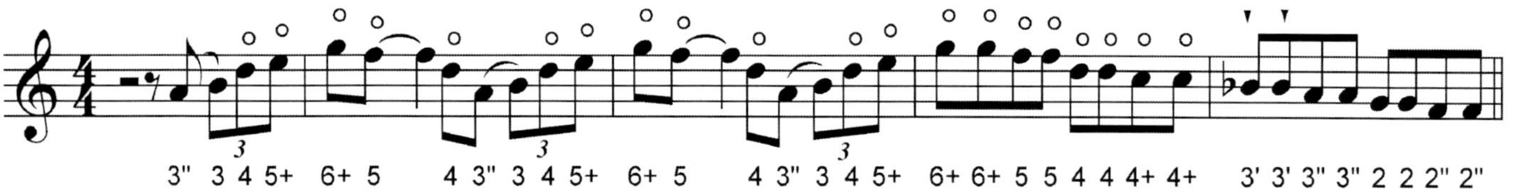

29 "Don't Fight It" by David Barrett

Key of Song: B-flat Major Tempo: ~200 Harmonica: A-flat Harmonica in 3rd Position (or E-flat in 2nd)

Groove: Swing Form: 12 Bar w/Alterations Instrumentation: Full Band

Chart: | **H** | **H** | Harp x3 | **H** | Gtr x3 | **H** | Drums x2 | **H** | Piano x3 | **H** | Organ x4 | Harp | **H** | **H** ||

Form: See head below.

Head

Drum Line #1 (first chorus of drum solo) – Track time: 2:19

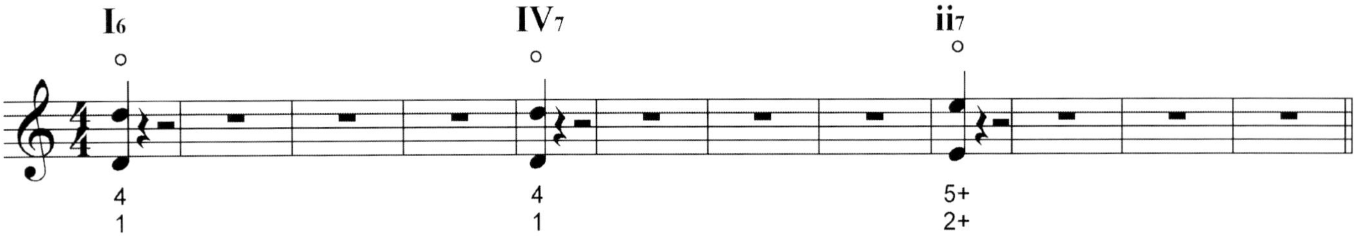

Drum Line #2 (second chorus of drum solo) – Track time: 2:32

30 "A Real Romance" by John Garcia

Key of Song: A Major Tempo: ~160 Harmonica: D Harmonica in 2nd Position

Groove: Swing Form: 12 Bar w/Alterations Instrumentation: Full Band

Chart: | Verse | Verse | Bridge | Harp Solo | Organ Solo | Guitar Solo | Verse | Verse | End ||

Hook – Track time: 0:15

Ending Line – Track time: 3:33

31 "Feelin' Good" by David Barrett

Key of Song: E Major Tempo: ~74 Harmonica: A Harmonica in 2nd Position

Groove: Shuffle Form: Standard 12 Bar Instrumentation: Guitar

Chart: | Harp Solo x5 | Harp Solo Break | Guitar Solo x2 | Harp Solo x2 ||

About the Author

David Barrett is the world's most prolific blues harmonica educator—leading the way in every facet of blues harmonica education for over twenty years.

The Early Years

Having played saxophone and trumpet as a youth, David already had a solid musical foundation before playing the harmonica at age fourteen. At age sixteen local harmonica legend Gary Smith took David under his wing as a private student. Gary also introduced David to the local blues jam scene and even invited him to participate is some of the local harmonica blowouts. By age eighteen David was studying music theory in college and started teaching harmonica at local music stores and institutes.

Author

By age twenty David had released his first book, Building Harmonica Technique, with one of the world's largest publishers, Mel Bay Publications. This book was the first serious blues harmonica method to be released in the market. David Barrett is now the world's most published author of blues harmonica lesson material, with over 60 book/audio sets and videos published.

David is also an active writer for various publications. David writes a featured column for Blues Revue Magazine called "Right On The Number" and is the editor and a writer for Mel Bay's www.HarmonicaSessions.com® and the Harmonica Masterclass Workshop Free eZine.

Workshops

David is the founder and head instructor of Harmonica Masterclass Workshops. Founded in 1994, the focus of these workshops has been to make quality hands-on instruction available to the masses. Classes range in size from 20 participants to 250 participants, depending on program type and location. David also employs the top educators in the world for these workshops, such as Joe Filisko and Dennis Gruenling, as well as top artists in today's blues harmonica music scene.

David also teaches, judges and performs at other prestigious events, such as Hohner's World Harmonica Festival and Steve Baker's Harmonica Masters Workshop in Trossingen, Germany.

Private Lessons

Since age eighteen David has been teaching blues harmonica lessons full-time. In 2002 David founded School of the Blues in San Jose, California—the first school in the world for the specific study of blues music. David and his instructors (Guitar, Bass, Organ/Keyboard/Piano, Vocals, and Drums) teach private lessons and workshops as well as fly-in lessons. David teaches on average fifty private students a month as well as home correspondence courses. David is also active in working with local hospitals, teaching his Harmonica for Fun & Health classes to people with COPD (Emphysema), asthma and heart disease.

Performing and Recording Artist

David is a Grammy Nominated blues harmonica player (for his work on John Lee Hooker Jr.'s album All Odds Against Me) and performs regularly in the California Bay Area (San Francisco Blues Festival, Monterey Bay Blues Festival, etc.) and abroad (Chicago, Germany, etc.). Recently he played as a featured artist in the Mark Hummel Blues Harmonica Blowouts, alongside James Cotton, Charlie Musselwhite, Kim Wilson, and Mark Hummel. David has recorded three albums, Serious Fun, We Are The Blues and the History of the Blues Harmonica Concert.

David has Worked or Played with:

Charlie Musselwhite, Mark Hummel, Lee Oskar, Rod Piazza, James Harman, James Cotton, Gary Smith, Andy Just, Mark Ford, Billy Boy Arnold, Jason Ricci, Rick Estrin, Paul deLay, Jerry Portnoy, Gary Primich, Howard Levy, Magic Dick, Tom Ball, Sonny Jr., John Mayall, Annie Raines, Paul Oscher, Phil Wiggins, Brendan Power, Sam Myers, Snooky Pryor, Steve Baker, Rob Paparozzi, Dennis Gruenling, Carlos del Junco, Mitch Kashmar, John Mayall, Joe Filisko, Lazy Lester, Kim Wilson, Kenny

Neal, Peter "Madcat" Ruth, Jr. Watson, Rusty Zinn, Nick Moss, Steve Freund, Johnny Cat, and John Garcia.

More Method Material by Author David Barrett

Harmonica Masterclass® Complete Blues Harmonica Lesson Series

Series 1 (Beginning)

1. Basic Blues Harmonica Method BK/AUDIO
2. Basic Blues Harmonica Method DVD
3. Blues Harmonica Jam Tracks & Soloing Concepts #1 BK/AUDIO

Series 2 (Intermediate)

4. Classic Chicago Blues Harp #1 BK/AUDIO
5. Blues Harmonica Jam Tracks & Soloing Concepts #2 BK/AUDIO
6. Scales, Patterns, & Bending Exercises #1 BK/AUDIO
7. Exploring 2nd Position BK/AUDIO
8. Exploring 3rd Position BK/AUDIO
9. Building Harmonica Technique DVD #1 & #2

Series 3 (Advanced)

10. Classic Chicago Blues Harp #2 BK/AUDIO
11. Blues Harmonica Jam Tracks & Soloing Concepts #3 BK/AUDIO
12. Scales, Patterns, & Bending Exercises #2 BK/AUDIO)
13. Exploring 1st Position BK/AUDIO
14. Basic Blues Chromatic for the Diatonic Player BK/AUDIO
15. Building Harmonica Technique DVD #3 & #4

School of the Blues Lesson Series

David is the author of all the harmonica books and coauthor of all these the other instrument books below

Special Focus

16. Improvising Blues Harmonica BK/AUDIO
17. Blues Harmonica Accompaniment Playing

Play-Along Trax

18. Blues Harmonica Play-Along Trax
19. Blues Guitar Play-Along Trax
20. Blues Keyboard Play-Along Trax
21. Blues Bass Play-Along Trax
22. Blues Drums Play-Along Trax

Method Books – Level 1

23. Blues Harmonica, Level 1
24. Blues Guitar, Level 1
25. Blues Keyboard, Level 1
26. Blues Bass, Level 1
27. Blues Drums, Level 1

Method Books – Level 2

28. Blues Harmonica, Level 2
29. Blues Guitar, Level 2
30. Blues Keyboard, Level 2
31. Essential Blues Bass Lines

More Method Material

Here are some more method books and audios from David Barrett

32. Building Harmonica Technique BK/AUDIO
33. Complete Classic Chicago Blues Harp BK/AUDIO
34. C Harmonica Blues Play-Along Tracks
35. First Lessons Blues Harmonica BK/AUDIO/VIDEO
36. First Lessons Harmonica BK/AUDIO/VIDEO
37. Blues Harp Licks Chart Bklt/AUDIO
38. Harmonica Position Chart
39. Harmonica Wall Chart
40. Youth Harmonica Method BK/AUDIO
41. Adult Harmonica Method BK/AUDIO
42. Harmonica for Fun & Health
43. Basic Harmonica Method BK/AUDIO
44. Gig Savers: Essential Harmonica Theory
45. Gig Savers: Essential Harmonica Scales
46. Gig Savers: Essential Harmonica Quick Charts
47. Gig Savers: Harmonica Microphones
48. Gig Savers: Harmonica Amplifiers
49. Gig Savers: First Harmonica Gig - Everything You Need to Know
50. Pocket Book Series: Blues Harp Classics Pocketbook
51. Pocket Book Series: Blues Harp Pocketbook
52. Fun with the Harmonica - AUDIO & VIDEO Only

Recordings

David Barrett is featured on the following recordings

1. *Serious Fun* – David Barrett & John Garcia (2003)
2. *We Are The Blues* – School of the Blues All-Star Band Live in the Studio (2005)
3. *History of the Blues Harmonica Concert* (2010) – With Joe Filisko, Dennis Gruenling, Kinya Pollard, Rusty Zinn, John Garcia and the School of the Blues All-Star Band